The Guide to

Selling Your Florida Law Practice

Ed Alexander, Esq.

The Guide to Selling Your Florida Law Practice

ISBN 978-0-9998936-0-9

Printed in USA by 48HrBooks (www.48HrBooks.com)

Praise for *The Guide to Selling Your Florida Law Practice*!

"The *Guide to Selling Your Florida Law Practice* is a true must-read for all solo and small firm practitioners. Dying at your desk is always an option, but not one that works to the advantage of your family. Instead, by using this guide you can maximize the return on your lifetime of hard work."

Peggy Hoyt, J.D. M.B.A., B.C.S,
Board certified Specialist in
Wills, Trusts, and Estates, and Elder Law

"Understanding and deciphering how much your law firm is worth is a difficult and complex task. You know it's more than just the furniture and computers, but you can't figure out how to account for those intangibles. Ed Alexander simplifies this process and shows you how to accurately estimate the *full* value of your firm. If you want to be an informed seller and make the choices that are best for you, you need to read this book!"

Patrick Wilson, J.D.
Sr. Practice Advisor, Atticus

Dedication

To Faith,

my best friend, love of my life, and wife of more than 33 years,

and Brittany and Courtney,

my smart, successful, and beautiful daughters.

Using This Guide

This Guide provides general legal information. It is ***not*** legal advice.

This Guide *does not create an attorney-client relationship* between the author (or Alexander Abramson, PLLC) and the reader (or any other person or entity).

The information in this Guide may not be applicable to your particular circumstances. Therefore, before you act on, rely upon, or utilize any of the information in this Guide, you should seek out professional advice tailored to your situation.

Neither the author nor Alexander Abramson, PLLC, make any representations or warranties whatsoever about the information in this Guide.

Table of Contents

ALEXANDER | ABRAMSON
BUSINESS LAWYERS PLLC

Welcome!

Dear Fellow Attorney:

Thank you for taking the time to get **The Guide to Selling Your Florida Law Practice**.

Every year, thousands of solo practitioners and small firm lawyers retire from the practice of law, but aren't sure how to sell and transfer their law firm. When I speak with my lawyer-clients, they tell me they've talked with their friends and it seems no one has a clear answer.

Rest assured that there is a path for you. By getting this guide, you've taken the first step toward selling your law firm so you can realize the value of your hard work and leave your firm, your clients, and the buyer in great shape.

You could have easily ignored this information and waited until your decision was forced. Instead, you were proactive and now have this resource.

Take **Gretchen,* a solo practitioner with two associates. Her practice had taken a hit during the Great Recession but survived** and was booming again. **Because of the drop in her retirement savings, she'd practiced longer than she wanted.** But the market had come back, and her revenues were higher than they'd ever been. She decided it was time to pull the trigger, but didn't know how to sell her practice.

Using the techniques discussed in this guide, **we worked with Gretchen to complete the sale of her practice to her associates**. She increased her retirement savings and gave her associates the opportunity to become law practice partners. Plus, she left the practice knowing that her staff and clients would be well taken care of. **Gretchen is now enjoying her new home in North Carolina.**

Gretchen is one of many lawyers we've helped transfer or sell their law practice. The past 24 years spent representing businesses and law firms has given me the experience to help guide you through the questions and issues that may arise in the sale of your law practice. This guide addresses common law practice sale issues to get you started down that path.

Once you've read this guide, please feel free to call me to discuss your situation. My hope is that you will look to us for help when you need it. We are excited to serve you.

Very truly yours,

Ed Alexander
Alexander Abramson, PLLC
Orlando

** The names and certain details of the examples in this guide have been changed to protect client confidentiality.*

Can You Sell a Law Practice?

The short answer is: *Yes.*

Whenever I hear this question—and I hear it a lot—I find it is really a combination of two questions:

Am I Permitted to Sell My Practice by the Florida Bar Rules?
and
Why Would Another Attorney Buy My Practice?

Do Florida Bar Rules Allow Me to Sell My Practice?

Yes. Florida Bar Rule 4-1.17 specifically contemplates and permits the sale of your law practice (or even a practice area). An in-depth discussion of the process, the requirements, and the steps to comply with Rule 4-1.17, as well as other Bar Rules that apply to the sale of a practice, is in the Bonus Material at the end of this guide. For now, though, just know that it is ethical to sell your practice.

Why Would Another Attorney Buy My Practice?

This is often the more difficult hill to get prospective sellers over. Another attorney will buy your practice because she can 1) make money from the firm and 2) use the firm income to pay you for the purchase. Plus, it's usually easier to step into an operating practice than it is to start one from scratch.

And though she's purchasing the entire practice, including the furniture, equipment, and ongoing matters, the real value of your firm to a buyer lies in its goodwill and intangibles, such as:

- The Likelihood of Repeat Business from Clients
- Relationships You and Your Staff Have Built with:
    - Clients and the Community, and

    - Referral sources

- Firm Name, Logo, and Reputation

- Firm Infrastructure, including:
    - Marketing Materials and Processes,
    - Client Intake and Engagement Systems,
    - Practice Management Tools and Software
    - Management Systems

- Trained, Experienced, and In-Place Staff

As long as there is a transfer of goodwill and intangibles from you to the buyer, the practice will be able to continue to operate as it has in the past, and the buyer will receive income from the firm you've grown and operated throughout the years.

Attorneys will sometimes tell me:

"There's no value in my firm because it's all intangible, just clients and my reputation."

Those attorneys are right about one thing: their firms are largely comprised of these intangibles. But they're wrong to think that these intangibles have no value. The value is in the firm's goodwill and intangibles.

In fact, today the biggest components of value of most businesses are goodwill and intangibles. According to *Ocean Tomo,* an intellectual property consulting firm, in 2015 87% of the value of the S&P 500 arose from goodwill and intangibles.[1]

---

[1] http://www.oceantomo.com/blog/2015/03-05-ocean-tomo-2015-intangible-asset-market-value/

What Does Selling Your Practice Look Like?

To fully describe the process of selling a practice, it is important to know the different ways you can leave your law practice, and which ones can lead to a sale.

According to singer-songwriter Paul Simon, there are '*50 Ways to Leave Your Lover*.' When it comes to a law practice, though, there are only four ways to leave, and only two of those ways can be used to sell a practice.

The Four Ways to Leave Your Law Practice:

- **'Die' at Your Desk**
- **Liquidate**
- **Internal Transfer**
- **External Transfer**

Let's take a look at each way to leave your practice and discuss the advantages and disadvantages of each option.

Die at Your Desk

Whether understood literally or metaphorically, in this scenario the lawyer works and manages the law firm until he can no longer work. This is the default method when a lawyer doesn't plan.

The main advantages to working until you can't are:

- No planning is required, and
- Earnings from your labor will continue until you stop working.

Of course, it's important to understand that physical and mental issues could prevent you from practicing long before you actually die.

The disadvantages, though, are many:

- Because it is unlikely that a firm can be sold after the lawyer dies, your family or heirs will never benefit from your hard work building the law firm.
- Because the work of the law firm stops suddenly, it is likely to result in the loss of most or all of the law firm's value—clients and employees aren't likely to hang around for weeks while things are sorted out by an inventory attorney.
- The burden of wrapping up the firm is pushed to others. An inventory attorney must settle your law firm's affairs and get things in order.
- Your employees are put out of work.
- Your current clients are left with partially completed work and have to look for new attorneys.
- Physical or mental limitations could make you have to stop working long before death, and the ability to sell at that time is substantially reduced.
- If your decline involves reduced mental capacity or dementia (happening often today with aging lawyers who practice long after they should have stopped, often due to financial reasons), you'll lose law firm income and value, and you might even be sanctioned or disbarred.

In short, *Die at Your Desk* is a risky proposition. You won't realize the value of the work you put into creating and building a law practice, plus it causes problems for clients, employees, and heirs. In my opinion, this should generally be avoided.

Liquidation

In this scenario, you, the retiring lawyer, pick an end date, close the practice doors, liquidate the practice assets, and pay the practice creditors. If there's anything left over once creditors are paid—and most often there isn't—it goes to you.

Often, a lawyer liquidating her practice must "run the practice out," meaning she continues to pay expenses during the time it takes to close up the firm without taking on new cases or having additional income. The practice can become a drain on your retirement account, rather than an income source, during this run-out period.

The advantage of this method is its simplicity.

Though some planning is required to ensure lease terminations are coordinated with the liquidation, shutting down your law firm and selling the assets can usually be done over a few months. After that you're free from the law firm and can enjoy retirement.

Destruction of the value of what could possibly be your most valuable asset is the primary disadvantage of liquidating your law practice.

In fact, I believe that:

Liquidating your law practice because you're retiring is like burning down your home because your kids moved out.

Most people would think that you'd lost your mind if you destroyed your home merely because you no longer needed the extra space. And yet, many lawyers see this as acceptable when it comes to retiring from their law practice.

About twenty years ago I had just started my law practice and was attending the local Bar luncheon. As chance would have it, I sat next to another attorney who also had just started his practice. As we were talking, this attorney said he'd just gotten a great deal on used furniture from a lawyer who was retiring. Knowing that I'd also just opened my doors, he let me know this retiring lawyer was also selling a law library.

Thinking that it would be much better to have more clients than more books, I called the retiring lawyer and suggested that, perhaps, I could buy both the law library <u>and</u> the law firm's client files. I told him that, since he wasn't going to be practicing any longer, I might be able to help those clients with future legal needs and grow my practice, and that I would, of course, be happy to pay him for both the files and the library.

Unfortunately for me (and for that lawyer, his staff, and his clients!), the concept of selling his practice was foreign to him—a bridge too far.

He claimed that what I was proposing was unethical and, despite me pointing out the Florida Bar rule permitting it, wasn't willing to change his position. He closed his doors and walked away from his practice. His employees were forced to find new jobs, and his clients were forced to find new lawyers. While he may have found good homes for the office *accoutrements*, the clients, the lifeblood of any practice, were left out in the cold.

This lawyer's reluctance to sell was due to his misconception that it was unethical for him to sell his firm. But more than that, I think, it stemmed from another, more pervasive misconception that law firms have no value beyond the office furniture and leather-bound books. I've had lawyers tell me: "Other than [my associate or law partner], who would be interested in my firm?" My experience suggests that for many firms the answer is "lots of people!"

The major disadvantage of liquidating a firm is that you lose all (or nearly all) of the value of your firm. Though you may be able to sell the desks, tables, chairs, computers, and other furniture and equipment (law library), you don't receive any value for the client relationships, referral arrangements, and other intangibles that you've worked so hard to develop and nurture.

Now, unfortunately, some lawyers have no other choice. Whether because of inaction, not understanding how to sell a firm, or poor management, many lawyers are actually forced into liquidation. A lawyer literally on the eve of retirement may try to sell a practice only to find out they don't have a saleable law firm or the time to market the firm.

According to a study conducted by the International Business Brokers Association, only 10% to 15% of all businesses that are offered for sale are actually sold.

> *This statistic is so depressing that many people have warned me against putting it in this book. But, I thought you should know what can happen—what does happen—in many cases when the process is taken for granted.*
>
> ***You* can avoid being part of that statistic through:**
>
> - *Advanced Planning* and
> - *Engaging Experienced Counsel Early in the Process.*

The reasons for this depressing statistic are described in detail below in "What Errors Do Attorneys Often Make When Selling?" For now, know that almost any law firm can become a saleable law firm, and we can help you get there. *Give us a call at 407-649-7777.*

The takeaway for these two methods of leaving your law firm is:

Dying at Your Desk or Liquidating Your Firm
Destroys the Value of Your Law Practice Asset.

Internal Transfer

With an internal transfer, a retiring lawyer transfers his equity to a partner or an associate. Based on my conversations with lawyers considering the sale of a practice, this is the most commonly desired option. They can be with or without consideration and for a fair price or a ridiculous price.

Bob and His Criminal Defense Practice
Take Bob, an extremely successful criminal defense attorney. He represented most of the high-profile criminal defendants in his local area, had an hourly rate that reflected his abilities, and logged many hours in the office. Bob loved to practice law and employed three other attorneys at his firm, two seasoned veterans and one "junior woodchuck" attorney.

Shortly after marrying for a second time, Bob decided he would retire in a few years to travel and spend time with his new wife. But, Bob was concerned. He didn't want to liquidate the firm and terminate his associate attorneys and staff. Yet, he wasn't sure the law practice could survive without him.

Bob brought in well over 80% of the billable work and was the face of the firm. Local news reporters knew him and many attorneys in town referred cases to Bob. In short, the firm was, like most solo and small firms, built around Bob and his capabilities and relationships.

Still, Bob had spent a lot of time and money building the firm and his reputation, and wanted to realize the benefits from that hard work. He wanted his associates to be successful and carry on the firm after he retired. To accomplish Bob's goals, we put in place a three-step process to transfer the firm to his two veteran attorneys.

First, the entire process was set out in a comprehensive contract that all parties signed. The veteran attorneys immediately became "partners" (shareholders) of the firm, each with a very small amount of equity to raise their status in the legal community. Bob then began the process of transferring his personal goodwill to the partners through a "team approach" and introductions.

Step two began two years later. Bob began a three-year semi-retirement phase, and the veterans bought additional equity of the firm to bring them to a 49% interest. This purchase was funded via a promissory note made by the buyers to Bob and secured by a lien on the law firm's equity.

During this time Bob worked from 16 days per month at the beginning to 4 days per month toward the end. Throughout he provided support to the buyers to transfer his personal relationships with referral sources and community members to them. Through his express confidence in the buyers and slow removal from the firm, he transferred his goodwill to the buyers.

In the fifth year, the veteran attorneys purchased the balance of Bob's equity and he fully retired. Bob continued to be available to them on a contract basis while he was traveling the world with his wife.

Internal Transfer Advantages

An internal transfer can work quite well for both the retiring lawyer and the buying lawyer. The existing relationship between the lawyers enables the retiring lawyer to better evaluate the buying lawyer to determine the likelihood of a successful transfer. And the experience in the law firm and with its clients and staff, enables the buying lawyer to complete a smooth transition of ownership, clients, and referral sources. In some cases, it also makes securing bank or SBA (small business administration) financing more likely.

An internal transfer can also be completed more quickly. Though the process implemented with Bob's firm took place over five years, you could complete an internal transfer in as little as one year.

Internal Transfer Disadvantages

Of course, nothing is perfect, and such is the case with the internal transfer. The biggest downside is that it is an *all-eggs-in-one-basket* strategy. If the transaction does not work, for whatever reason, you'll have to work for a while to find another buyer and retire. And there will be negative effects on your firm's performance and employees from a failed internal transfer.

Mitigating this downside requires time: time to get to know the new buyer professionally and personally, to see how he performs as a lawyer and as a business person and how he deals with clients and others.

Other disadvantages of an internal transfer include:

- Your associate or partner may not have the assets to make a down payment, or the credit to secure a loan. Without cash ("skin in the game") or financing, or both, an internal transfer becomes risky for you. Selling to a buyer who doesn't have assets at risk in the purchase will not be successful most of the time. It will be too easy for the buyer to leave when a cash flow crunch happens or other problems arise.

- Your associate or partner may not be qualified to run the law firm. Training an employee to be a law firm owner is an involved process that can take some time to complete. Some buyers may never be able to fully make the leap, resulting in the ultimate failure of the internal transfer.

- A limited pool of buyers (i.e. only your associate or partner) could likely result in a lower price. If there's only one deal to be had, it may not be favorable to the party who wants or needs the deal the most. You might be forced to accept unreasonable terms to get the deal done.

External Transfer

With an external transfer, the law firm is marketed and, ultimately, sold to an unrelated third-party lawyer or law firm (e.g. as an office expansion). You've probably seen ads for practices offered for an external transfer sale in the *Florida Bar News.* To complete an external transfer, the best course of action is to engage a business broker to market your firm who understands the unique aspects of selling a law practice.

Kim had a real estate practice with a co-located title company. She was the only attorney in her practice but had many competent title closers, a paralegal, and a clerical support person. It was a thriving practice.

After finding and buying her retirement home in another state, Kim set a goal of selling her practice and retiring fully in two to three years. With no internal buyer possible, Kim engaged us to list and market her practice.[2]

We marketed the practice to lawyers and title insurance companies. There were several offers on the firm in short order, and Kim closed the sale less than five months from the listing date. She received an all-cash deal with an escrow hold-back and was required to work in the firm full-time for three months and part-time for the next nine months, receiving an hourly rate for the time she devoted to the business. She remained 'on call' to address issues by telephone for a year afterward.

After her year of full- and part-time work requirements, the buyer rarely contacted her. She was able to sell the firm and fully retire within her two-year window.

External Transfer Advantages

Assuming your law firm is properly marketed to a pool of potential buyers, the primary advantage of this option is that it typically results in the highest purchase price. Though you will be expected to stay on with the law firm for a time, you will have a known end date and be able to cleanly move into retirement.

Another advantage of the external transfer is focus. Because you have advisors working on your behalf to market your practice, you

---

[2] I am part owner of a business brokerage, FitzGibbon Alexander, Inc., in addition to my law practice.

can focus on keeping the law practice going and growing. If you lose focus and the revenues or profitability of your firm declines, it will become less valuable and more difficult to sell. Keeping your law firm on track is crucial.

Of course, an external law firm sale requires strict adherence to the Florida Bar Rules, including Rule 4-1.17 (described in detail in "Key Florida Bar Rules that Impact the Sale of Your Law Practice", in the *Special Bonus Material* at the end of this guide).

External Transfer Disadvantages

There are disadvantages to an external transfer as well.

- Costs of Transfer. The costs of an external transfer are, on the surface, higher than the internal transfer because they include the broker's commission and lawyer and accountant fees.

  I say "*on the surface*" because the realized expense of the broker's commission may actually be lower.

  - The International Business Brokers Association (IBBA) reports that business owners realize approximately 20% more for a business when an IBBA Certified Business Intermediary (CBI) broker represents the seller. If, in fact, you receive twenty percent more for your law firm, the benefit of the increased purchase price would far exceed the costs of using a broker.
  - It is difficult for you, the seller, to chase a prospective buyer without looking desperate. A perception of desperation means a lower purchase price. A broker, on the other hand, is expected, and in fact obligated, to pursue prospective buyers. So there's no impact on the seller or the price.

- Marketing your practice and dealing with inquiries from prospective buyers (and tire kickers) is a full-time job. You already have a full-time job running your practice. If you lose focus on that job, revenues and profitability are likely to suffer. You don't want to go into a sale transaction when revenues or profits have recently dipped because any decline during the sale process will have a disproportionately negative impact on the price and your ability to sell.

- Time. An external transfer is not an overnight process and requires upfront planning. The *median* time to sell a business through a business broker is between 9 and 12 months, assuming it is properly priced and marketed. For a law firm, though, the time frame may be longer. Often there are matters to be cleaned up or improvements to be made, and you'll need to stay with the firm after the sale to complete the transfer. Therefore, you should keep in mind that an external transfer will likely be a multi-year process. But with proper planning, you can avoid this pitfall entirely.

- Negotiation and Stress. Negotiations associated with a sale can be extremely stressful. Sale transactions can run the gamut from simple, straight-forward purchases to intricate transactions filled with hours and hours of negotiation. The benefit of avoiding any additional stress during an already stressful process, cannot be overstated. Using an experienced business lawyer and business broker will minimize your stress through experiential knowledge and strategy.

The bottom line is that, with an external transfer done properly, a lawyer realizes the maximum value for the practice.

How Much is Your Practice Worth?

Before we get into this topic there are a few things we need to be clear about.

First, this section isn't going to make you a valuation expert. This is an area that is full of mathematics and theories and, like the practice of law, proficiency can only be had with many years of training and experience.

Instead, the goal is for you to be able to establish a "ball park" estimate of the value of your law practice. To get there without much complication, I'm going to take some short cuts that could disturb valuation professionals. This is a 30,000-foot overview of the process.

Second, this is an estimate, not a valuation. True *fair market value* of an asset isn't fully and finally determined until a willing buyer and a willing seller, both with full knowledge of all facts and circumstance and neither under any compulsion to sell or buy, complete a transaction for the sale of the asset.

Of course, that isn't very helpful for you when you merely want to know what you can expect if you sell your practice.

What we're looking to get close to—and what brokers usually establish when they complete an opinion of value to list a business for sale—is the "most probable selling price," which I'll refer to as the Value Estimate*.[3]

Third, this process necessarily involves numbers. Hopefully, you'll just be transferring numbers from your firm's financial statements.

[3] Definitions for the terms with an asterisk can be found in the Glossary.

But if that isn't the case, I encourage you to speak with your accountant or bookkeeper to get the numbers you need. This exercise is worth going through both for the process itself and for arriving at the end result.

Finally, the Value Estimate is determined without including real estate that is owned by your firm. We'll discuss how your firm owning real estate can affect the value below. But, the value of the real estate will be determined separately from the value of your practice.[4]

Now that that is out of the way, let's get to it.

At the most basic level, a buyer of your firm is buying the income stream your firm will produce in the future, and she will pay you for that income based on general interest rates and the risks associated with your firm.

Therefore, **the Value Estimate of your practice is determined by two factors**:

- The *"Income"* of Your Practice, and
- The likelihood that the "Income" will continue into the future (or, alternatively, the risk of it decreasing or stopping).

First, we're going to walk through practice income and how it is 'adjusted' for valuation purposes.

---

[4] If you want to 'geek out' on this issue, the reason is that the risk of owning real property is much lower than the risk of owning a small business.

Then, we'll take a look at some rules of thumb (that indirectly address the risk component) and, using the adjusted practice income, arrive at the Value Estimate.

Practice Income

The income of your practice that's used to determine practice value (called Discretionary Income*) is different than the net income shown on your firm's profit and loss statement (the P&L Income*) and on its tax return. Adjustments are made to the P&L Income to arrive at the Discretionary Income of your practice. This is the "income" that is used when determining the value of your practice.[5]

For example, lawyers, like most business owners, have discretion on how they spend the revenues that come into their practice, and they usually want to reduce their tax burdens by reducing the income for tax purposes.

Discretionary Expenses* do just that, reduce the taxable P&L Income. These discretionary expenses are business expenses that provide benefits to the lawyer or his family but do not have to be continued by a buyer of that practice.

For example, you might elect to attend an ABA conference in Hawaii one year or travel to Europe for a CLE seminar. Or, you could purchase a luxury automobile that you drive on firm business and pay for through your firm.

None of those expenses is required to make your practice operate. If you decided not to attend the conference or CLE seminar, your practice wouldn't suffer. If you used a non-luxury automobile to go

---

[5] Discretionary income is used for practices where the gross revenues are less than $1.5MM to $2MM. Above that the earnings before interest taxes, depreciation, and amortization (EBITDA) is more typically used.

to hearings or meetings, your practice wouldn't suffer. Yet, most or all of these expenses are tax deductible as valid business expenses.

You may also have expenses that are not being paid at a market rate, called underpaid expenses. For example, if your spouse works as your firm administrator or bookkeeper or computer technician, but you pay no salary for that position, a buyer would have to fill that role after the purchase. For those types of expenses the "income" of your practice would be decreased by the market value of those services to reflect the costs a buyer would incur to secure those services after the sale.

Of course, normal expenses—those that are necessary for the operation of the firm—are not used to adjust P&L Income. These include salaries, taxes, and insurance for your staff and associates, as well as rent, office supplies, marketing and advertising, and other similar expenses.[6]

Discretionary Earnings

To determine your firm's Discretionary Earnings—**the "income" of your practice upon which to base a value estimate—**it is necessary to determine the P&L Income of your practice after adjusting for:

- Discretionary Expenses,
- Underpaid Expenses,
- Financing Decisions and Costs (c.g. interest expense),

---

[6] But note that some expenses that are considered "normal expenses" may become partially discretionary and be part of the adjustments to P&L Income. For example, if you've employed your legal assistant for the past twenty years and are paying her a salary that is above the market rate, then the salary in excess of market would be a discretionary expense as long as it wasn't necessary to keep her employed with the firm post-sale.

- Taxes, and
- Deductions for Depreciation, Section 179 Expenses, and Amortization*.

Categories of discretionary expenses that are added to net income include:

- Travel and Entertainment for the Owner-Lawyer,
- Automobile Expense for the Owner-Lawyer,
- Cell phone for the Owner-Lawyer,
- Salary for the Owner-Lawyer[7]
- Family Salaries (for no-show or overpaid positions),
- FICA, Medicare, Health and Life Insurance, and Pension Contributions for the Owner-Lawyer,
- Rent for Real Property Owned by the Owner-Lawyer that is above a Market Rental Rate, and
- Charitable Contributions.

The following types of expenses are also added to P&L Income:

- Bad Debts and Refunds,
- Depreciation and Amortization,
- Interest Expense and Interest Income,
- Extraordinary Income (e.g. you received a referral fee in a personal injury case and don't normally practice personal injury law),

---

[7] Of course, many lawyers just pay themselves what is left over. If this is the case for your firm, then the entire amount of your compensation will be added here. If, on the other hand, you pay yourself a salary and make distributions of profits on a quarterly basis, then your salary would be listed here.

- Equipment Leases, and
- Taxes.

Categories of underpaid expenses that are deducted from P&L Income include:

- Rent for Real Property Owned by the Seller where the Rent is Below Market Rate, and
- Family Services Provided to the Law Practice at No-Cost—with the actual cost for the Buyer to secure the services being deducted from P&L Income.

> *If this process seems a little complicated to you, don't worry, you're not alone. I'm always happy to sit down with an attorney like you to personalize this information and put it in the context of your firm's situation. Give me a call at 407-649-7777.*

Calculating Discretionary Income for Your Practice

Now that you know the basic types of adjustments that are made to P&L Income to arrive at the Discretionary Income, it is time to apply these to your practice.

To help you do this without too much pain, I've provided a *Law Firm Discretionary Income Adjustment Worksheet* at the end of this guide that will allow you to calculate to your firm's Discretionary Income.

All you have to do is print your law practice profit and loss statement for the last fiscal year and fill in the blanks on the worksheet.

If an adjustment isn't shown on your firm's profit and loss statement and you can't find it, just take a reasonable guess. You can always update it later. For the payroll taxes on your salary, which probably won't be separately stated, just use 7.65% of your salary.

> *Special Note.*
> *To arrive at the best estimate of your firm's value, it can be helpful to look at (and most valuation professionals use) a weighted average of Discretionary Income (DI) over a three- to five-year period. This will give you a more complete picture of your law firm's performance.*

Law Practice Value Estimate

Rather than take you through a calculation of risk based on PhD level mathematics skills, we're going to look at:

- Rules of Thumb for law practice valuation, and
- Factors that will help you apply them to your practice.

Then we'll tie everything up with a quick "reality check" of your value estimate.

Please remember, this is just an estimate. The result a broker would establish when undertaking an in-depth review to establish a most probable selling price could be quite different from the rule of thumb estimate because of factors and issues that are particular to your practice and beyond the scope of this guide.

Practice Value Rules of Thumb.

The value of your law firm will be between:

- 0.5 and 1.0 times Gross Revenue*,[8] and
- 1.0 and 4.0 times Discretionary Income.

---

[8] Gross revenue should exclude any revenue that is outside of your normal practice area or arises from a special activity (e.g. referral fees for personal injury cases when you don't practice in that area).

At first, you may be thinking, "The range of these two multipliers is way too wide to be useful."

Fortunately, I will show you in the following section how to determine, based on a number of criteria, where your firm lies on the Gross revenue scale and on the Discretionary income scale. For this to be accurate, though, you must do one thing: BE HONEST!

You might also be wondering whether to use the gross revenue multiplier or the discretionary income multiplier.

The answer is: you should use both! The result of each calculation individually is useful, but more significant is what we can learn from comparing them. We'll discuss this in more detail later in "What if Applying Both Rules of Thumb Gives Wildly Different Values?"

Practice Characteristics and Performance Impact the Rules of Thumb

Determining value, even when it's an estimate, isn't merely a mechanical application of numbers.

In fact, two practices that have the same gross revenue or discretionary income can have very different values. What separates those values is the risk of the income continuing after the sale. And that risk is determined by the characteristics of the practice as well as its historical performance.

Take, for example, two law firms with annual revenues of $1MM and a lawyer-shareholder net of $300,000. The first is an estate planning firm that generated its revenue from 25 new client matters at $25,000 gross per matter, with the balance coming from work for past clients (i.e. repeat business).

The second is a litigation firm that generated its revenue from 12 cases, primarily from two key clients, who together account for 70% of firm revenues.

Though each firm has the same revenue and has repeat client business, all other things being equal, the estate planning firm is worth much more than the litigation firm because the risk of the revenue going away is much lower for the estate planning firm. It has a larger number of clients (but not too large) in addition to the repeat client business. If this firm loses a couple of clients, its overall profitability isn't destroyed.

On the other hand, the risk of the revenue going away is much greater for the litigation firm because it gets its business primarily from two clients, and the average case represents slightly more than 8% of the firm's total gross revenue. The firm has a high client concentration and a high revenue-matter concentration considering its total gross revenues. If this firm loses a single client, it will suffer nearly a 10% loss to its profitability. If two or three of its cases are resolved and not quickly replaced, the firm profitability will be severely impacted.

Though these rules of thumb are based numerically on gross revenue and discretionary income, the hidden component is the 'riskiness' of your firm. Risk is evaluated using a number of criteria, including the factors describe above and the performance of your firm. The descriptions below will help you decide what values on the gross revenue and discretionary income scale best represent your firm.

> *It is very important to keep in mind that where your firm's value estimate falls on the rules of thumb is* ***not*** *a reflection of your skills as a lawyer. The rules of thumb merely reflect*

how the practice generates revenue and whether, without you being part of the firm, that revenue will continue.

The *mid-range values* of the rules of thumb (.75 times gross revenue and 2 times discretionary income) would suggest a *typical* firm in terms of risk and performance.

So, what is a *typical* firm and how do you know if your firm is one? Typical firms have all or some of the following characteristics:

- In existence for five years or more,
- Profitability of 20%–30% of gross revenue (after normalizing your salary to that of a senior associate),
- Revenue per employee (including staff) of $220,000 or more,
- Experienced and properly compensated staff,
- Rent expense of not more than 10% of gross revenue, and
- Marketing expense of not more than 5% of gross revenue.

The value estimation process can make people feel like they're drowning in numbers and details. If your head is spinning right now, don't throw in the towel. I'm happy to sit down with you to walk you through this process one-on-one, and answer all of your questions. Call me at 407-649-7777.

Most firms will be in the mid-range of value. If you don't know whether your firm is mid, high, or low, use can use the mid-range values of the rules of thumb.

The high-end values of the rules of thumb (1.0 times gross revenue and 3 to 4 times discretionary income) assume your firm is better than typical, much better.

This can be the case where there is a large amount of recurring business, a marketing system that is not dependent solely on the owner-lawyer, and a low level of client concentration. In fact, all other things being equal, the less involved the owner-lawyer is in the firm prior to the sale—other than, perhaps, serving some of the clients—the more likely the firm is better than typical for purposes of valuation.

Very few firms will be in the high-end range of value for the rules of thumb. If you decide this is appropriate for your firm, you should have specific reasons you believe this is the case.

Finally, the low-end values of the rules of thumb (0.5 times gross revenue and 1 times discretionary income) assume your firm has a few problems. Perhaps profitability is lower than expected, you have few or no staff, or you're working 50 to 60 hours a week to make a small profit.

If this is the case for you and you have time, you will be better off fixing the problems and running the firm for a few more years before you sell. Plus, many a dissatisfied attorney has rediscovered his love of the law once the practice is back on track.

What if Applying Both Rules of Thumb Gives Wildly Different Values?

The results of both calculations should be in the ballpark of one another. If the value derived from the multiplication of gross revenue far exceeds the value derived from the multiplication of discretionary income, your firm may not be profitable enough. If, on the other hand, the value derived from the multiplication of gross revenue is below the value derived from the multiplication of discretionary income, your firm may be running too lean.

If the numbers vary wildly, you should compare your firm's performance to the benchmarks given above and fully understand where and why it is different than the typical or high-performance firms.

Knowing where you stand today is essential to setting realistic expectations for the sale of your practice.

Reality Checking Your Practice Value Estimate

One way to do a reality check on the estimated value of your practice is to put yourself in the buyer's shoes. Bottom line, your practice must pay for itself through the discretionary income it will generate for the buyer. This exercise puts your Value Estimate to that test.

The Reality Check Worksheet below will show whether your practice generates enough income to cover the debt service necessary to pay a loan the buyer would use to acquire your practice, taking into account a reasonable down payment by the buyer and a reasonable salary for the buyer.

There's one thing you must do for this worksheet to work for you. You must be honest and realistic with the both the buyer salary and the working capital*. It is unlikely that a buyer will take less than a normal salary to buy your practice, and working capital requirements aren't going to suddenly fall once you sell. The practice will, hopefully, operate the same after you sell.

> *Special Note*
>
> *A good way to estimate working capital is to take the total cost to operate your practice for a month (excluding your salary) and multiply it by the number of months on average it takes your firm to collect invoices.*

Reality Check Worksheet[9]

	Amount:	*Notes:*
1) Estimated Firm Value:		
2) Cash Payment:		*Min. of 5%, 25% typical.*
3) Law Firm Working Capital:		*Two to three months expenses, depending on collection period.*
4) SBA Guarantee Fee:		*Estimate this as 2.7% of line 1 minus line 2, plus line 3.*
5) Amount Financed:		*Line 1 minus line 2, plus line 3 and line 4.*
6) Interest Rate:		*6.5 to 9% as of Q1, 2018*
7) Debt service: Principal and Interest payment on line 5.		*Assume monthly payments amortized fully over seven years. Go to* http://www.calculator.net/loan-calculator.html *for a loan calculator*

	Amount:	*Notes:*
A) Discretionary Income:		
B) Buyer Salary:		*Equivalent to a senior associate.*
C) Net Available for Debt Service:		*Line A minus line B.*
D) Debt Service		*The amount from line 7 above.*
E) Debt Service Coverage Ratio		*Divide line C by line D.*

Banks look for the Debt Service Coverage Ratio* to be between one and two. If your calculation is below one, the price is too high. The buyer won't be able to afford your practice. If it is above two, you're leaving money on the table.

---

9 To receive a preformatted Excel spreadsheet for all the worksheets in this Guide, go to http://www.practiceexits.com/DIworksheet and sign up now.

Where Do You Start?

First, decide on your time frame. The earlier you start, the better.

You'll want to have a minimum of two to three years to complete a sale. If your time frame is greater, you'll have more flexibility and the opportunity to pivot if something goes wrong. Some attorneys I've worked with have planned as many as ten years in advance!

If you need to sell immediately, your options are more limited. A one-step internal sale can be accomplished in the least amount of time if all the conditions are right—e.g. your internal buyer can finance the practice, you and she agree on the firm's value, and you believe that she has the professional and business expertise to run your firm successfully. Similarly, a profitable practice that's in good shape can be marketed and sold externally between nine months and a year after it is listed.

Second, determine if your firm's Value Estimate is in line with your goals and financial requirements.

Determine a Value Estimate for your firm as described in *How Much is Your Practice* Worth?

If that Value Estimate isn't where it needs to be, determine the critical performance factors that need to be improved to increase discretionary income and decrease risk. Then, single out those that you can resolve within the time you've allotted for your sale. Again, more time usually means a better overall increase in value.

Be sure you identify any 'low hanging fruit', meaning improvements to a firm that are relatively easy and quick to implement but that can have big impact on value. As a rule, more marketing effort, increasing rates, establishing better client selection criteria, all have the effect of reducing the number of clients and increasing the profitability of each client (i.e. more profitable cases). More profitable cases increase discretionary income and, all other things being equal, the overall value of your law firm as well.

> *If you're not sure what to do, I can help you develop an improvement plan or put you in touch with people who have a track record of helping lawyers improve their firms. I am a resource for you through this process. Call me at 407-649-7777.*

Occasionally, an attorney looking to sell improves her practice to a point that she finds renewed joy in the practice of law and wants to continue practicing rather than sell.

Third, think about who might be a good buyer. This will help identify what sale strategy to initiate.

Finally, call us at 407-649-7777! Whether your sale is on the horizon or still years away, we can offer valuable information and guidance at all stages of the selling process. Take the next step and begin these conversations now so that we can set you on the right path to a trouble-free and profitable sale.

What Errors Do Attorneys Often Make When Selling?

Not Having Enough Time

Your ability to complete a sale at a reasonable value is very much dependent on the time you have to complete the sale. Time, here, can be your enemy or your friend.

In fact, I would argue that you can't start this process too soon. My experience has shown me that there is a direct correlation between the amount of time you leave to plan and execute the sale and the net sale proceeds you'll receive at the closing. Less time usually equals less money.

If your time to complete the sale is short, you're going to be at the mercy of the buyer. Because you can't walk away from the deal, but the buyer can, the buyer is in the driver's seat and can force a purchase price well below market value. In other words, the value of the firm becomes what that buyer is willing to quickly pay.

Plus, knowing you have get your deal done quickly puts you at an emotional disadvantage. When your future is tied up in a practice sale transaction that must be done soon, the stress can be extreme.

I encountered one case a few years ago where both time and the number of buyers were a problem. Bill's co-shareholder, John, was appointed to high public office. Knowing his official duties would begin at the start of the calendar year and that he had only few short months to divest himself of his law firm, John approached Bill about buying John's stock. John suggested a pricc that seemed fair based on what he and Bill had created. Bill said that he'd "think about it," but that he wanted to see how things progressed before coming to any arrangement.

The weeks passed, and each time John raised the topic of the buyout with Bill, he would respond that he still needed to "think about it." By Christmas John was getting desperate and, rather than worrying about getting a fair price, he just wanted to avoid getting nothing. Bill finally made a low-ball counter-offer after Christmas which John immediately accepted. The sale closed just before New Year's Eve.

John's need to sell in a limited time frame hurt his bargaining position and resulted in him receiving a price for his part of the law firm that was well below what he believed it was worth.[10] John also ran into the problem of limiting himself to an internal transfer, thereby minimizing his pool of buyers. We'll look specifically at the "single option" problem in the following section.

Of course, this situation isn't limited to partnerships. It can also occur with an internal transfer to an associate or even an external sale.

In fact, whenever a lawyer delays planning and implementing an exit from her law practice, she is turning time against her.

Adequate time also provides one additional benefit: the opportunity to fix problems. Most firms aren't perfect and have a few things that should be fixed or improved. These fixes can yield significant benefits, both in firm income (and lawyer stress reduction) and in overall firm value.

---

[10] I would also argue that John's failure to have a proper buyout process detailed in the firm's partnership agreement also worked against him. For more on partnership agreements, you can see my upcoming "Guide to Partnership Agreements."

To avoid paying the full retail price, I knew I had to create an option that wasn't this car, and I had to make that the option credible to the salesman.

Many attorneys encounter this "single option" problem when they limit the sales process to an internal transfer to an associate.

First, if the lone buyer for the practice believes it is not worth what you think it's worth, you're not going to get a deal closed or you're going to sell at a lower price than you want.

The best scenario for you, the seller, is for there to be multiple offers. The prices and terms of those offers will ensure the highest likelihood that the practice will sell at fair market value to a qualified buyer.

Therefore, you must have (or manufacture the credible appearance of having) multiple options. This, of course, doesn't mean *lie* about having additional offers. Instead, keep yourself open to multiple selling options.

Second, if the only buyer doesn't have the financial wherewithal to secure bank financing, you'll be left to finance the entire practice purchase. And while seller financing is typical in business sale transactions and you should expect to hold paper* (a promissory note from the buyer) from your sale, why would you want to make a loan for a large amount of the purchase price when a bank won't take that risk?

Multiple buyer options increase the likelihood that:

- You'll receive an appropriate price for your firm,
- You'll receive more cash at the closing, and

You must allow for adequate time to complete a sale, to cc alternatives to an internal transfer, and to make quick fixes. V too long can lead to a hurry-up-have-to low price transaction

Having One Option

A mistake closely related to time is having only one option f sale.

When my daughter was a freshman in college she wanted a wife and I agreed to buy her one if she completed two big go the summer between her freshman and sophomore yea completed them in record time and began the search for he car.

As luck would have it, she found one of her dream cars fc Orlando at a local dealership. We drove to check it out ar seeing it, she gushed (right in front of the salesman, no less is exactly what I want!" I think I saw him smile.

Knowing that I didn't have an alternative, I created one. I salesman that my wife and I were not sold on this model we were looking at other safer and more fuel-efficient m We left the dealership saying we were going to look at othe would get back with them.

A couple of days later, I called the dealership back. After tel we were still looking at other cars and that my wife and I we this car because it wasn't a top safety pick, I suggested a m price. They countered, and we eventually came to a deal. I paid a little more than I should have in the end, but my dau happy.

- The transaction will actually close.

Trying to "DIY"

My 24 years of experience have proved to me that trying to transfer your practice by yourself will cost you more money and take more time than engaging qualified and experienced professionals from the start.

As you know from practicing law, there are always nuances and little bits of information and experience that you use to shape an outcome for a client. In your practice area, you know when something is a great opportunity, even when it may not look that way to your client, and when there is reason to be cautious. You know how things work, when you can push, and when you shouldn't push.

Just imagine how you'd respond to a potential client who, after meeting with you and getting some basic legal information, says, "Thanks anyway. I think I can take care of this case on my own." You may wish him the best, but you doubt it will turn out that way.

> *There's proof that the adage "A little knowledge is a dangerous thing" is true.*
>
> *Known as the Dunning-Krueger Effect (for which Dunning and Krueger won an "Ig" Nobel Prize), research has shown that people of low ability in a particular subject matter consistently overestimate their competence because they misperceive their ability in the subject matter relative to the ability of others. They confuse information about the subject matter with depth of knowledge and experience in the subject matter.*

> *My observational experience suggests that those who are very intelligent are more susceptible to the effect.*
>
> *Interestingly enough, the effect works in reverse too. You may have given a legal task that you thought was simple to an associate, paralegal, or legal assistant, and that person just couldn't perform the task. In that situation, you misperceived how easily the task could be completed because you are fully competent at it.*

The bottom line:

Even though you're a smart and successful lawyer,
you shouldn't try a DIY practice sale.

Specific reasons to use a business lawyer who is experienced with law practice transfers (and, for external transfers, a competent and trustworthy business broker) include:

- **Reality**: This practice is your baby and that means the transfer process will be full of emotions. As you know from your practice, decisions made when emotions are running high are typically not the best decisions.

  Experienced and trustworthy advisors get beyond the emotion and bring reality to your situation in many key areas, including:

  - *Pricing*. A practice, like a house, that is priced too high won't sell. Period. And, after it's on the market for a while with no sale, brokers and prospective buyers will assume it has major problems. As time passes, the seller becomes desperate and willing to take a low-ball offer when it comes along.

***Beware!** There is an entire cadre of brokers who will list businesses at unrealistic prices desired by their owners just to get the listing. These (in my opinion, dishonest) brokers know the overpriced businesses won't sell, but they want the listing for two reasons.*

First, they'll advertise the listing to get prospective buyers to call. When they're talking with a prospective buyer, they'll suggest she consider another reasonably priced business.

Second, they'll go back to the owners five or six months later to "improve the listing" (i.e. to pressure the seller to reduce the price). The broker typically says something to the effect of, "the market is telling us your business isn't worth the listing price." If the broker gets the seller to drop the price to a realistic price, it may sell. Meanwhile, the seller has lost six months, and the business may be tainted in the market.

As a resource for you through this process, I'd be happy to suggest an experienced and effective business broker who will act ethically for you. Just call me at 407-649-7777.

- *Terms*. Sellers always want an all-cash deal, paid in full at the closing table. However, when a seller isn't willing to hold paper on a portion of the purchase price, the transfer will take longer (if it sells at all) and the firm will sell at a lower price.

  External brokers can assist with setting realistic terms, especially for an internal transfer where the pre-existing relationship can muddy the business aspects of the transaction. Trust must be supplemented by documented arrangements protecting both parties according to the deal terms.

  - *Negotiation*. You need someone else to be the bad guy. I'm sure you've done it for your clients—I've done it for mine. Whether it's being the guy who says "no," delivers the bad news, or whom the client throws under the proverbial bus to preserve a future relationship, the value of a competent business lawyer in the thick of negotiation cannot be overstated. And it's not only being the "bad guy" or coming up with alternatives, having a business lawyer spearhead the negotiation makes the process much less stressful for the owner.

- **Buyer Relationship**: As I've shown in this book, the ability to effect a sale requires a transfer of goodwill and intangibles from you to the buyer. If that relationship is diminished because of negotiation or "chasing" the buyer to move the ball forward, the post-closing transfer will be difficult and uncomfortable.

  Moreover, you will need a great relationship with the buyer at closing and right afterward because you'll have to transition clients and referral sources, and because things will inevitably come up that will stress that relationship in the future. Starting out at less than good is not desirable.

- **Confidentiality**: Maintaining confidentiality is difficult, if not impossible, to do when you're DIYing a practice sale. If this is important for your transaction, engaging counsel and a business broker will be a requirement.

- **Chasing a Prospective Buyer**. There may come a time in the process when you'll have to push a prospective buyer to secure an offer or, hopefully, to get the buyer to increase an offer in light of other higher offers (i.e. multiple offers). It is difficult, if not impossible, for you as the seller to push a prospective buyer for an offer without looking desperate. Business brokers and counsel, on the other hand, are expected to push and, sometimes, cajole prospective buyers into making an offer.

DIYing your practice sale might seem, at first blush, a good way to save money. But it causes problems that can actually cost more money and could cause the transaction to take more time or crater entirely.

The Professional Liability Insurance Blunder

Protecting yourself against a professional liability claim that is made after a sale is crucial. During your time practicing you likely have maintained professional liability insurance to protect yourself. After the sale, though, that policy may be terminated and not cover you.

Most professional liability policies today are "claims made" policies. To be covered by such a policy, a claim must be both (1) based on a situation that occurred while the policy was in force, and (2) be made against the firm while the policy is in force.[11]

Now, you might be wondering what happens when a firm changes policies for a better rate or terms. To get firms to change, insurance companies will often provide coverage for claims based on situations that occurred prior to the start of the policy through a "retroactive

[11] Some policies have extended reporting period ("ERP") provisions that will provide extended coverage for a retiring attorney without requiring an additional premium. Often, the policy must have been in force for a specified period of time (three or five years, for example). You should be sure to read your firm's policy or contact your broker to determine if you have that coverage.

date." The retroactive date creates a fiction that the policy was in effect earlier than it was. This means that the firm (or a particular attorney within the firm) is covered for a claim made during the actual time the policy is in effect for any situation occurring on or after the retroactive date.

Once a policy is terminated, it will not cover claims, even those where the situation arose after the retroactive date. Therefore, if the buyer terminates your prior policy and doesn't maintain the same retroactive date for you on her new policy, you won't be covered for the same acts that were covered under your prior policy.[12]

Since you will likely not want to go without coverage after the sale, you have two primary options.

The first is to purchase tail coverage from your current insurer. Tail coverage* insures you for claims that arose when the policy was in force (including the retroactive period) but weren't made until after the policy terminated. Though this is the best alternative for a seller, the premium can be expensive.

The second alternative is to require the buyer to maintain a similar policy—amount of coverage and maximum deductible—with the same retroactive date as your current policy (for you), and have the law firm indemnify you for claims made after the sale.

Determining which option is best depends on:

- The cost of tail coverage,
- The structure of the purchase and whether the buyer will continue with the same law firm entity or not, and

---

[12] For certain purchase structures the buyer may not be able to cover you, even if she wanted to do so.

- Whether you will be employed by the law firm after the sale.

How professional liability insurance is to be addressed must be incorporated into the purchase contract and in place at the closing. Without addressing it specifically, you could find yourself having to pay a tail coverage premium from the sale proceeds.

Special Bonus Material

Key Florida Bar Rules that Impact the Sale of Your Law Practice

Rule 4-1.17

Florida Bar Rule 4-1.17 specifically contemplates and permits the sale of your law practice (or even a practice area). The comments to the rule include the statement:

> *The practice of law is a profession, not merely a business. Clients are not commodities that can be purchased and sold at will. In accordance with the requirements of this rule, when a lawyer or an entire firm sells the practice and other lawyers or firms take over the representation, the selling lawyer or firm may obtain compensation for the reasonable value of the practice as may withdrawing partners of law firms.*

The bottom line is: if you follow the specific steps required by the rule, you can sell your law practice. But, as you can imagine, the steps required by the rule are detailed and lead to a few questions and issues.

In addition, the contract for the sale of your practice must take into account your obligation and those of the buyer under the rule (and the Bar Rules in general).

First, as would be expected, your <u>buyer must be authorized to practice law in Florida</u>. This can be easily verified at the outset.

Beyond verification, however, the purchase contract should include a provision directed to the buyer's status as a lawyer in Florida, and that there are no pending disciplinary actions against him.

Next, you must provide written notice to your clients stating:

- There will be a sale,
- The client has the right to retain another lawyer if they choose, and
- If the client does not object within 30 days of receiving the written notice, the client's consent to substitution of the buyer as the client's attorney will be presumed.

Of course, those are the minimum provisions. There are no prohibitions on providing more information, and I strongly suggest you provide information about the buyer, your availability to the client during the transition, and a statement that there will be no increase in costs to the client as a result of the sale.

The sale cannot be closed until after the 30-day notice period.

If you don't receive the return receipt for a client (i.e. you don't have a good address for the client), then there are two courses of action available to you. For matters that don't involve pending litigation, the matter cannot be included in the sale. For pending litigation matters, you must secure an order permitting the substitution.

Also, if a client objects to substitution of the buyer as her new counsel, but the client does not secure alternative counsel, and you do not want to continue representing the client, you'll have to withdraw as you normally would (in accordance with Rule 4-1.16).

For pending litigation matters, court approval is required for the substitution of the buyer as the client's counsel.

Therefore, if you do close just after the 30-day notice period, some matters may not be included in the sale at that time.

The 30-day notice requirement also means that, now that you're thinking of selling your practice, you should:

- Maintain an accurate computerized database of client contact information (this can be used for marketing purposes as well),
- Use an engagement agreement that, among other terms, includes an obligation for the client to keep you informed of their contact information,
- Don't let matters linger: send a matter closing letter to each client promptly upon the conclusion of your work for that client (your professional liability carrier will love you for this too), and
- Don't let trust account deposits remain in your trust account any longer than necessary.

Text of Rule 4-1.17 - Sale of a Law Practice.

Rule 4-1.17 Sale of a Law Practice

A lawyer or a law firm may sell or purchase a law practice, or an area of practice, including good will, provided that:

(a) Sale of Practice or Area of Practice as an Entirety. The entire practice, or the entire area of practice, is sold to 1 or more lawyers or law firms authorized to practice law in Florida.

(b) Notice to Clients. Written notice is served by certified mail, return receipt requested, on each of the seller's clients of:

(1) the proposed sale;

(2) the client's right to retain other counsel; and

(3) the fact that the client's consent to the substitution of counsel will be presumed if the client does not object within 30 days after being served with notice.

(c) Court Approval Required. If a representation involves pending litigation, there will be no substitution of counsel or termination of representation unless authorized by the court. The seller may disclose, *in camera*, to the court information relating to the representation only to the extent necessary to obtain an order authorizing the substitution of counsel or termination of representation.

(d) Client Objections. If a client objects to the proposed substitution of counsel, the seller must comply with the requirements of rule 4-1.16(d).

(e) Consummation of Sale. A sale of a law practice may not be consummated until:

(1) with respect to clients of the seller who were served with written notice of the proposed sale, the 30-day period referred to in subdivision (b)(3) has expired or all these clients have consented to the substitution of counsel or termination of representation; and

(2) court orders have been entered authorizing substitution of counsel for all clients who could not be served with written notice of the proposed sale and whose representations involve pending litigation; provided, in the event the court fails to grant a substitution of counsel in a matter involving pending litigation, that matter may not be included in the sale and the sale otherwise will be unaffected. Further, the matters not involving pending litigation of any client who cannot be served with written notice of the proposed sale may not be included in the sale and the sale otherwise will be unaffected.

(f) Existing Fee Contracts Controlling. The purchaser must honor the fee agreements that were entered into between the seller and the seller's clients. The fees charged clients may not be increased by reason of the sale.

Rule 4-5.6: Restrictions on Practice

In a typical business sale, the selling business owner agrees not to compete against the buyer for a period of time, often as much as five years. Though disfavored at common law, Florida has a statute (Section 542.335) requiring courts to enforce non-compete agreements and other restrictive covenants as long as they meet certain criteria.

This makes sense. No one would buy a business only to have the seller open a competing business a few doors down the block or call on customers of the business that was sold.

However, in the case with lawyers, Florida Bar Rule 4-5.6 prohibits a lawyer from entering an agreement that restricts the lawyer's right to practice after employment or partnership has ended, and in other situations.

Luckily, in the case of the sale of a law practice, that restriction is lifted. The comment to Rule 4-5.6 provides an exception to the rule in the case of the sale of a practice undertaken in accordance with Rule 4-1.17.

Therefore, you can legitimately enter a non-compete agreement with the buyer and, as a result, maximize the value of your practice.

Rule 4-1.5(g): Ethical Implications of a Price Based on Future Law Firm Revenue

Often a buyer will propose an "earn-out" as a means to properly price a law firm. With an earn-out the buyer pays the seller a percentage of the fees received from the clients of the seller's law firm for a specific period of time (e.g. two or three years), instead of a single fixed payment.

Earn out arrangements are sold as "fair" because the buyer is only paying for the clients that move to the new firm.

However, there are two problems with earn-out arrangements in law firms.

First, all of the risk of the price is borne by the seller. If the buyer doesn't manage the practice well or fails to adequately market, the seller suffers the consequences. Years of hard work building a client base and referral source goodwill can be lost over a short period of time. And when the practice has been sold, there's no chance to rebuild it.

Second, if the seller is not going to work for the buyer's firm for the entire period of the earn-out, then seller and buyer must comply with Rule 4-15(g), in order to be able to split the fees.

Rule 4.15(g) permits fee division between lawyers not in the same firm only if:

- The total fee is reasonable *(already required by Rule 4-1.5(a))*,
- The division is in proportion to the services performed by each lawyer,
- The client agrees in a writing that fully discloses the division and the basis for the division, and

- Both lawyers are jointly responsible and available to consult with the client.

Obviously, this rule presents problems for both the seller and the buyer. It is unlikely that a seller, who is not not employed by the law firm after the sale, will perform services for the firm's clients, will want to be jointly responsible for firm matters, or will consult with the firm's clients.

This means that, if an earn-out is part of the deal terms:

- The seller must <u>remain employed</u> by the law firm after the sale,
- The amounts paid to the buyer must be specifically allocated between compensation for the lawyer's work on firm matters, and purchase price for the firm (which will likely be treated more favorably for tax purposes)
- There must be a written employment agreement for the term of the earn-out,
- There must be a liquidated amount payable by the buyer if the employment is terminated before the end of the term to ensure the purchase price is paid, and
- The buyer must be obligated to maintain a minimum amount of professional liability insurance (with a maximum deductible).

Other Bar Rule Questions and Issues

Unfortunately, I don't have the room in this guide to address all of the Bar Rules and related issues that affect the sale of a law practice.

The Rules give rise to many questions that should be discussed with your attorney:

- When preparing for a sale,

- Before signing a listing agreement with a broker (if you're completing an external transfer), and
- Before you sign a contract for sale.

Some of these questions include:

- When does an internal transfer become subject to Rule 4-1.17?
- Who must receive the Rule 4-1.17 notice?
- What information about clients and cases can you provide to the prospective buyer before the closing?
- What obligations do you have concerning past client files and information?
- What are your ethical obligations to "investigate" your buyer?

These may apply depending on the process you'll be using to complete your sale, and may require specific language in your sale agreement.

Law Firm Discretionary Income Adjustment Worksheet

Your Law Firm Name:	
Year of Income Adjustment:	
P&L Net Income:	$
Adjustments	
Additions:	
Interest Expense	
Tax Liability (of Law Firm)	
Depreciation and Sec. 179 Exp.	
Amortization	
Travel and Entertainment	
Automobile	
Cellphone	
Excess Family Salaries	
Owner Salary and Bonus	
Owner Payroll Taxes	
Owner Health Insurance	
Owner Retirement Contributions	
Charitable Contributions	
Bad Debts and Refunds	
Equipment Lease Payments	
Excess Rent Payments	
Other:	
Other:	
Total Additions:	$

Continued on next page…

Deletions:	
No-Cost Family Services	
Below Market Rent Payment	
Interest Income	
Extra Ordinary Income	
Other:	
Other:	
Total Deletions:	$
Law Firm Discretionary Earnings	$

Conclusion:
A $500,000 Warning
Before You Go Back to Your Normal Work

Thank you for taking the time to read this guide. I hope you found it helpful. Implementing the information from this guide will help you avoid a situation I hear about regularly.

A while back I spoke with an attorney who was thinking about selling his practice. He had a good-sized practice with qualified staff and regular clients, and he earned a respectable income. His health had begun to deteriorate, and he knew he'd have to retire in a few short years. Based on the information he provided during our call, I roughly estimated that the practice would be worth $500,000 to $600,000.

During our call, he told me that the sale process seemed stressful and that he'd never had a colleague who sold a practice. He then told me that he'd received an offer from a large firm to merge his practice into the large firm. He was seriously considering the offer because all he had to do was move his practice to the firm and continue to work for the next few years until he was ready to retire.

I asked whether he would receive cash or a signing bonus at the time of the merger. The answer was "no."

I asked whether he would receive a buyout when he decided to retire. Again, the answer was "no."

Why, I wondered, would this attorney be willing to throw away a $500,000 asset? Why did he fail to realize the value of the practice that he'd managed, grown, and operated for so many years?

You now know that selling your law practice will enable you to realize the value of your hard work. Though you collect fees for the day-to-day work, the long-term monetary benefits of building and managing your practice can only be realized if you sell. And those benefits (the sale proceeds) can change your life.

You probably won't be able to retire on the value of your practice alone. But that extra cash could mean a comfortable retirement full of the activities you enjoy.

Of course, as you can see from the information presented in this guide, selling isn't automatic. But a successful sale can be accomplished by:

- Planning Ahead: It is never too early to begin the process.
- Knowing What Your Practice is Worth: Understanding how the value of your practice is determined can help you understand how to increase its value through risk reduction or income increases, and plan appropriately.
- Engaging Qualified and Experienced Advisors: This isn't a DIY process, and trying to DIY it can cost you. Plus, experienced advisors will probably pay for themselves through increased deal value and security.

My hope is that you will turn to us for help when you're ready to start the process. We're here to help you. If you have any questions about your practice, the process or completing a sale, just call me at 407-649-7777.

I look forward to talking with you.

Ed Alexander
407-649-7777
Ed@AlexanderAbramson.com

Glossary of Terms

Amortization: The fixed repayment schedule of the principal of a loan.

Debt Service Coverage Ratio (DSCR): Measurement of the firm's ability to generate enough cash flow to cover its debt payments.

Debt Service: The cash that is required to cover debt payments in a specific time period.

Discretionary Expenses: Any cost that is not essential for the operation of the law firm.

Discretionary Income (DI): Incoming remaining after all essential business costs have been taken into account. DI is a measure of the firm's performance after tax planning of the owner.

Extended Reporting Period (aka Tail Coverage): A designated period after a claims-made policy has expired during which a claim may be made and coverage triggered as if the claim had been made during the policy period.

Gross revenue: Sales income from all client payments, fees, and other sales of the law firm.

Holding paper: When at the time of a sale, the seller accepts a secured promissory note (the "paper") for all or part of the purchase price, with payments occurring over an agreed upon period of time.

Law Firm Working Capital: Cash required to meet payroll and pay other operating expenses for a given period of time.

Profit and Loss Statement: A financial statement that summarizes the revenues, costs, and expenses during a specific period of time, usually a fiscal quarter or year.

Value Estimate: The expected value of your law firm after accounting for DI and the risk of the DI continuing into the future.

Weighted Average: An average in which each quantity to be averaged is assigned a weight. The weight determines the relative importance of each quantity.

The Author: Ed Alexander

Ed Alexander is a business lawyer focusing on multi-owner business and professional practice transactions and arrangements, including:

- ❑ Creating lasting and profitable partnership arrangements, including partner add-on transactions.
- ❑ Partner dispute resolution.
- ❑ Transitioning business and practice ownership through asset and equity sales and purchases.
- ❑ Developing franchise and business system licensing arrangements.
- ❑ Equity financing through private placement transactions.

Ed is admitted to practice in Florida (1993) and New York (1994) and has been a business attorney since becoming a lawyer. Ed is also a licensed business broker and principal of FitzGibbon Alexander, Inc. He is the author of

10 Common and Costly Business Killing Legal Mistakes and How to Avoid Them.

A Business Law Bible for Entrepreneurs.

Prior to becoming a lawyer, Ed held positions in the tech world and has been part of teams that designed software and hardware for the first generation of defibrillator pacemakers, as well as custom analog and digital integrated circuits used in automobiles and healthcare applications. In 1995, Ed was **awarded U.S. Patent, No. 5,468,952**, for the 1992 invention of a combined miniature laser scanner and portable handheld computer. This invention is still in use today in gift registry applications for retailers.

In 2015, Ed received the *Partner Award from the University of Central Florida Business Incubation Program* for his more than fifteen years of service excellence to the program. In 2014, Ed received the Orange

County Bar Association *Judge J.C. "Jake" Stone Distinguished Service Award* for his 18 years of *pro bono* work as a volunteer guardian ad-litem for abused and neglected children. In 2013, he was awarded the *Small Business Development Center Regional Volunteer of the Year Award*.

He also enjoys travel and outdoor activities including mountain biking, kayaking, hiking, and sailing.

